Use this Trip Journal to plan
your trip and record your

Write a packing list

Things to do before leaving

Things to see

What to avoid

Record the weather

Daily Journal

Stick in photos & tickets

WALK ON THE WILD SiDE

Name:

Trip Date:

I'm Travelling With

_____

_____

How I'm Getting There

_____

_____

Where I'm Staying

_____

_____

I'm Excited About

_____

_____

Packing List

Things to Do Before Leaving

_____

_____

_____

_____

_____

_____

_____

_____

_____

_____

_____

_____

_____

_____

I'm Planning to See...

I'd Like To Avoid...

The Journey

I Saw...

I Heard...

It Was Funny When...

The Food...

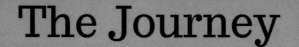

The Best Part Was...

Daily Journal

Date: _____   Location: _____

What we did today:

_____

_____

_____

_____

_____

_____

Weather: _____

Favorite Food: _____

Rate It: ☆ ☆ ☆ ☆ ☆

GiRAFFES

ZEBRAS

SAFARi TOURS

LIONS

Daily Journal

Date: _____   Location: _____

What we did today:

_____

_____

_____

_____

_____

_____

Weather: _____

Favorite Food: _____

Rate It:

Daily Journal

Date: _____   Location: _____

What we did today:

_____

_____

_____

_____

_____

Weather: _____

Favorite Food: _____

Rate It: ☆ ☆ ☆ ☆ ☆

Daily Journal

Date: _____   Location: _____

What we did today:

_____

_____

_____

_____

_____

_____

Weather: _____

Favorite Food: _____

Rate It: ☆ ☆ ☆ ☆ ☆

Daily Journal

Date: _____   Location: _____

What we did today:

_____

_____

_____

_____

_____

Weather: _____

Favorite Food: _____

Rate It: ☆ ☆ ☆ ☆ ☆

Daily Journal

Date: _____   Location: _____

What we did today:

_____

_____

_____

_____

_____

_____

Weather: _____

Favorite Food: _____

Rate It: ☆ ☆ ☆ ☆ ☆

Daily Journal

Date: _____   Location: _____

What we did today:

_____

_____

_____

_____

_____

_____

Weather: _____

Favorite Food: _____

Rate It: ☆ ☆ ☆ ☆ ☆

Daily Journal

Date: _____ Location: _____

What we did today:

_____

_____

_____

_____

_____

_____

Weather: _____

Favorite Food: _____

Rate It: ☆ ☆ ☆ ☆ ☆

GiRAFFES

ZEBRAS

SAFARi TOURS

LIONS

Daily Journal

Date: _____   Location: _____

What we did today:

_____

_____

_____

_____

_____

_____

Weather: _____

Favorite Food: _____

Rate It:

Daily Journal

Date: _____ Location: _____

What we did today:

_____

_____

_____

_____

_____

Weather: _____

Favorite Food: _____

Rate It: ☆ ☆ ☆ ☆ ☆

Daily Journal

Date: _____   Location: _____

What we did today:

_____

_____

_____

_____

_____

_____

Weather: _____

Favorite Food: _____

Rate It: ☆ ☆ ☆ ☆ ☆

Daily Journal

Date: _____ Location: _____

What we did today:

_____

_____

_____

_____

_____

Weather: _____
Favorite Food: _____

Rate It: ☆ ☆ ☆ ☆ ☆

Daily Journal

Date: _____   Location: _____

What we did today:

_____

_____

_____

_____

_____

Weather: _____

Favorite Food: _____

Rate It: ☆ ☆ ☆ ☆ ☆

Daily Journal

Date: _____   Location: _____

What we did today:

_____

_____

_____

_____

_____

_____

Weather: _____

Favorite Food: _____

Rate It: ☆ ☆ ☆ ☆ ☆